PERSONAL INTERVIEW MODULE

A2Z HANDBOOK SERIES

ATTITUDE MATTERZ

Copyright © Attitude Matterz
All Rights Reserved.

To all the Attitude matterZ students who requested and encouraged us to compile our Personal Interview Training & Placement workshops in a book so that it could reach millions of job aspirants out there who are preparing for upcoming interviews!

Contents

Foreword

Since the time I had known Farheen at Tata Motors Limited where she was my colleague, I had seen her too obsessed and immensely passionate about trainings and personality development guidance to college students. She is one amongst the very few trainers who has the power to rule the crowd- all her students have only praised her; I knew for sure that this lady would do something miraculously big and with her strong leap with Attitude matterZ, I am sure she would impact millions of students' lives and will help them in realising their dream careers.

When I read this book, I was surprised to see such a valuable collection of preparatory answers for Personal Interview. Not only the questions have an answer, but also the reasonings as to why the question is asked- none of the personal interview books that I have read so far has this!

This is a must to read books for all pre final, final year students as well as fresh graduates out of college and have started their career. Can't wait to read more A2Z series handbooks lined up.

I wish Farheen and the entire mentor team at Attitude matterZ a very good luck in their journey of making students more employable.

Shreya Agrawal,
Manager@ Flipkart
Ex- Tata Motors Limited
MBA: IMT Ghaziabad

Preface

A2Z Handbook on Personal interview is the first book in the A2Z Placement Preparation Series. It is a complete preparation guide written, compiled, and edited by IIMs/ FMS/ SP Jain/ IITs/ BITs/MDI/NITs Alumni. I tried including all the tips and tricks that we teach our students during our workshops. 75% of the interviewers say that "How" you answer during interviews matters much more than "What" you answer.

This is the main reason that we have compiled industry accepted answers for Top 50 Interview Questions. After reading this book, you will be able to tackle any personal interview of any company with ease. It is advised to prepare your own answers in a separate notebook once you finish reading this book.

All the Best for your upcoming interviews.
Land up to your dream job!

Acknowledgements

I would like to thank the entire mentor pool at Attitude matterZ, for helping in refining the contents of the book and in framing the industry standard answers which ha sthe potential to help millions of job aspirants. Special Thanks to Akshay Mhole, sales manager at Tata Motors, Ashish Ambastha, SDE III at Flipkart, Muaz Hyder, consultant at Bain & Co., Smriti Kumari, SDE II at Amazon, Rashmi Rani, I.A.S. 2021, Saumya Singh, Area Manager at Pepsico, Narendar Lamba, Intelligence Officer- GOI, Prof. Abhishek Srivastava, IIM Vishakhapatnam, Amrita Sneha, Manager at SBI and many others who have helped in curating and refining the contents of the book.

I would also like to thank 8Tudem Tech. Pvt. Ltd. for providing this opportunity and sponsoring the book so that the book could reach the masses. The images in the book are taken from www.freepik.com.

Last but the most important of all- the entire student community of Attitude matterZ who requested and encouraged me to write the training contents in the form of a book.

Thank You All!

About The Company

Attitude matterZ is a unit of 8TUDEM TECH PVT. LTD., a Government of India recognized start-up.

We are dedicated towards serving students to land up to their dream career by assisting them via our placement preparation modules, supporting working professionals via our upskilling courses and partnering with companies to provide digital marketing services. We extensively conduct workshops-seminars at premier institutes across India. All our workshops are conducted by IIM/ ISB/ XLRI/ MDI/ FMS/ IIFT/ IMT Alumni only.

Our mentors works at top-tier firms including Google, Facebook, Amazon, BCG, Goldman Sachs, Big 4, TATAs and many more. With this book we plan to compile our trainings in the form of a single book.

We believe that there is practically no end to learning - but given the time constraints and the competition in this generation - you must learn and prioritize only what is the need of the hour. Come and enjoy to be a part of our success community.

A2Z Handbook Series

A2Z Handbook series is our dedicated book series for placement preparations. We have similar A2Z handbooks on Group Discussion, Guesstimates, Consulting Case preparation, Digital Marketing and many more.

Feel free to reach us @www.attitudematterz.com & info@attitudematterz.com

From The Director's Desk

Mr. Tanmay Raj is a young and budding entrepreneur who has laid the foundation of two companies.

Tanmay believes in continuous learning for everyone including himself. Currently, Tanmay has been enrolled in Executive Digital Marketing and Entrepreneurship Program at The Wharton School, University of Pennsylvania.

Tanmay holds an Engineering degree from Aryabhatta Knowledge University, Patna, an MBA degree from NIT Kurukshetra and an Advanced degree in Digital Marketing from IIM Jammu. Tanmay has worked and collaborated with esteemed companies like Genpact, Toyota, LiuGong, Tata Steel Aashiyana, PepsiCo (VBL) and has a rich experience in framing digital marketing strategies for MSME clients.

Tanmay is rightly known for his networking and leadership skills. He is presently a member of International Youth Council, United Nations and has been elected as the General Secretary and Vice President at various clubs and societies. Prior to Attitude matterZ, Tanmay has co-founded a startup namely Business garage which aimed at providing digital marketing strategies to MSMEs.

Tanmay has a vision of spreading quality education for all at a nominal cost.

CHAPTER ONE

Question Bank

Top 50 questions from 8 categories: frequently asked by top companies		
S. No.	**Category**	**Question**
1		Tell me something about yourself.
2		Describe yourself.
3		Tell me something which is not there in your resume. (Accenture)
4	About You	What is the meaning of your name? (Byju's)
5		Tell me about yourself as a professional /a friend/ a son/ or a daughter.
6		Tell me about your family. (IndiaMART)
7		What should be your 'Epitaph'? (Tata Steel)
8		What motivates you? (Goldman Sachs)
9	Your	What are you passionate about? (Google)
10	Personality	What are your biggest strengths?
11		What are your weaknesses?
12		Where do you see yourself in the next five years?
13		Where do you see yourself in the next ten years?
14	Hindsight/ Leadership skills	Who is your role model? Why do you admire him/ her? In what way are you similar to your role model? (Tata Power)
15		Why should I hire you? Why do you think you are a good fit for this role?
16		Have you led a team before? Also, are you a Team Player OR a Team Leader? (Byju's)

S. No.	Category	Question
17	Your Interests/ achievements	List your hobbies and interests. (Flipkart)
18		List all the extra-curricular activities that you have ever participated in and mention awards.
19		Explain your project/ internship that you have done so far. (Flipkart)
20		What have you done so far for the society? (ONGC)
21	Behavioural questions	How do you typically respond to problems? (These problems could be in any sphere of your life)
22		Give instances where you took charge of a difficult situation and resolved it. (Amazon)
23		What was the toughest decision you had to make? OR What was the toughest challenge you had to take up and how did you go about it? (Google)
24		Describe one incident or event where you initially stumbled, but eventually recovered and were able to achieve your objectives. (Amazon)
25		Imagine a situation that you have a priority task lined up. How will you accommodate the task given that you already have list of tasks lined up for the day? (Directi)
26		What would you do if you are not selected?(Yes Bank)
27		What is your plan B if you don't get selected in the entire campus placements? (HUL)
28	Negative questions	Why do you have such poor grades/ academic performance? (BCG)
29		What you do not like about this college? (Wipro)
30		What you did not like about our company?
31		Where do you think is the present Govt is lacking? What would you have done different if you were in that position? (TAS)

S. No.	Category	Question
32	Your Preparedness	Have you gone through our (company's) website? What do you know about this company? (Emami)
33		What do you know about this Industry? (HUL)
34		What do you know about the Job Description?
35		Why do you want to join our company?
36		Why do you want to join this role? OR is this role aligned to your career objectives? Please explain how?
37		Why did you choose to do MBA?
38		How do you plan to learn this skill (could be a software/ digital marketing/ coding,etc) since you do not know about it? (Disney)
39		Why should I hire you and not others? (McKinsey)
40	All time favourite questions	What is consulting? (Deloitte)
41		Why do you think are consultants paid so high?(BCG)
42		What is the difference between marketing and sales?
43		What is the daily revenue of Business Standard?
44		Marketing plan: Share me a plan to sell 100 units of baby food online. (Moglix)
45		Your Client is the owner of automobile dealership in Delhi and is expecting flat sales. Find reasons and give recommendations. (Bain & Co.)
46		How will you rate yourself as a 1) planner 2) executioner?
47		What is MBA in Operations?
48		How important do you think is digital marketing for our business?
49		Do you have any questions to ask me?
50		What is your salary expectation?

CHAPTER TWO

What is a Personal Interview?

We will start with the introduction of personal interview so that you have some clarity beforehand on why exactly a personal interview is conducted as a final leg in entrance exams and recruitment process. Personal Interview is "a meeting that is organised by the recruitment team **to evaluate potential employee** with respect to a **fitment in the job vacancy and organization culture.**"

Now let us break it down into parts and understand it in this manner:

Imagine there is a set up- a table or office desk where on one side we have the person who will be taking your interview (who is called as an **interviewer**) and on the other side (usually the opposite side) it would be you who will be giving the interview (and you are called as an **interviewee**).

A usual Interview Set-up

It is to be noted that:

- there can be one or more person who can take your interviews
- your interviews can have multiple rounds

Focussing back to the definition- personal interview is a short meeting organised by someone in the recruitment team of the hiring company. The objective of the hiring company is to look for "people" (**potential employee**) who can do the given piece of job (fill the **vacant job position**) for them. The interviewer will have to do some sort of assessment to evaluate the potential employee for his fitment both for task/job and fitment in organizational culture.

A candidate who is being interviewed is broadly evaluated along these two aspects-

- **Your present job skills**- Does the candidate's skillsets even matches with the skills that the company requires? for example, if there is a vacancy for market research, it is important to check that does the potential employee can even do market research OR has this candidate done some sort of an internship earlier which involved a bit of market research (& hence internships are so important) OR how interested is the candidate for this particular job profile (which is the profile of a market research analyst)
- **Organizational fitment**- This second aspect is generally overlooked by candidates. Organizational fitment is many a times more important for giants like Amazon, Google, TATA, etc. This aspect tells the interviewer how well this person fits into the overall company's fitment. For example, if you are getting interviewed for the TATA and somehow even a tinge of arrogancy or a compromise on ethics is observed during your interviews, however good a candidate you would be, you will get rejected. The interviewer checks whether the candidate is qualified /under qualified/ overqualified for working in the kind of team setup that the company has.

Whenever you are giving an interview make sure that the above two aspects are in line with your resume, your body language and the kind of answers that you give.

All The Best!

The Hiring Process

In this section we will discuss about the hiring process of a fresher in individual college, in a pool interview and process for experienced working professionals.

RESUME SCREENING	01
WRITTEN ASSESSMENT ROUND	02
GROUP DISCUSSION ROUND	03
PERSONAL INTERVIEW ROUND(s)	04

Most Common Hiring Process

The above infographic depicts the usual hiring process. There can be one or multiple rounds during Personal Interviews depending upon the company's policy and in many companies, you may not have all the above four stages, for example, there might be only GD and PI. But for a well-prepared candidate, all four stages are a must. For example, if you only prepare for GD and PI and let's say Google visits your campus and calls in application for written assessment, you cannot go and say "Conduct GD instead of Written assessment because I have not prepared it."

A good cricket player knows how to hit ALL Shorts!

The Resume Selection:

The first step begins with the screening of the candidate's resume as per job skill sets and list of past engagements (co -curricular/ internships/ work experience). This step is ignored by not only the students but working professionals too! Answer me a question, if you are rejected in round 1 only, what is the use of preparing for rounds 2, 3 and 4? Always remember, your resume is your first face (first impression) to the company- when a recruiter sees your resume, he sees a part of you and creates a mental perception about you. By looking at your resume for 20-30 seconds only, he would decide which 50% of the candidate would move ahead with the process and which 50% would be stopped here itself.

In the words of Afan, Manager, HR- Sony Ericson, *"The recruiter is a gatekeeper, and your resume is an entry ticket to the show- and this gatekeeper checks and validates certain points in your resume and only if you meet those criteria he will give you a gate-pass to the next level."*

Screening Applications

Remember the **objective of this stage is rejection of candidates**. To quote in the words of Priyanshi, recruiter at Make My Trip, recruiter or interviewer thinks- *"I focus on rejecting most resume applications so that I am left with only the quality ones!"* Your race of being in the quality pool of students begins right here. At Attitude matterZ, we have a separate 1.5-hour session on resume building, selection and guidance to understand what are the different elements that should be added into a resume as a student and how healthy, attractive and ATS friendly (for keywords) we can make a resume so that it gets shortlisted end of the day.

The Written Assessment:

Once you have made your way through the resume screening, you enter to the second part of show which is 'The written assessment test'. Note that this can be optional for some of the companies but generally when the number of students is high, especially during hiring in engineering colleges, this process becomes crucial, so the objective of recruiter here again is **"rejection of candidates and filter the quality ones from the crowd"**.

Why is written assessment so important in college placements?

Most of the students in the batch have ~80% things similar in their resume. To understand the technical skills and logical ability of various students (apart from college grades), companies conduct written assessment to filter out the top 10 or 20 percentile students from the entire batch.

<u>UNDERSTANDING THE INTERVIEWER's MINDSET</u>

Consider a scenario where there are 100 students who are participating in the written assessment test and as a recruiter, I only want 2 or 3 people to join my company, so I will go forward with a written assessment test to eliminate 75 students and proceed with top 25 students (as a recruiter, I only have few hours to hire the right candidate from a vast pool of applicants).

These top 25 candidates will now move to group discussion (GD) round. Basis GD rounds, I will then select 8-10 candidates for the final interview and based on the interview performance I shall finally select 2 to 3 candidate and extend the job offer. This is the usual ratio of selections in each round. Hence it is important to ensure that you pass the written assessment test.

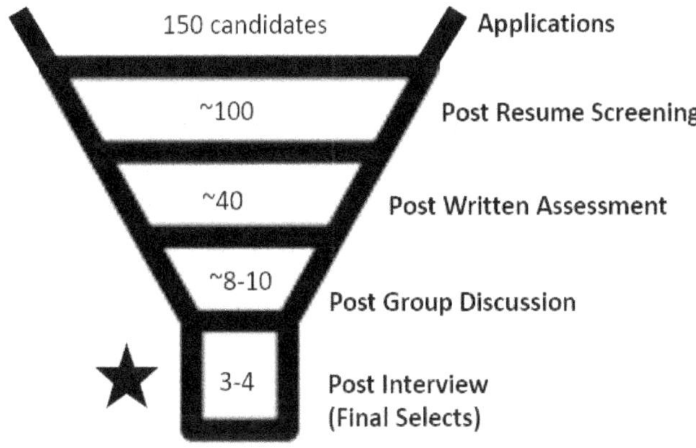

Usual Campus Placement Hiring ratio*

**As per the Survey of 50 recruiters in Tier 2 and 3 colleges for BBA, MBA and Engineering*

This test could be a mix of objective reasoning questions, aptitude questions, it could be some technical questions (let's say if you have a background in finance it could be some questions on interest, loans, laws, etc. if you're sitting for a consulting interview they might ask you to solve a short case study, undergo a short simulation game - anything that showcases your ability to read and interpret a lot of data points). So, you need to practice aptitude, last year's question pattern (get hold of your seniors who have made it to these companies).

"ALWAYS BE IN TOUCH WITH YOUR SENIORS WHO HAVE MADE IT TO THESE COMPANIES"

The Group Discussion:

The 3rd leg is Group Discussion (GD) which is often ignored in terms of practice by the students. Students prepare a lot for individual interviews and forgets that apart from individual personality traits, the team behaviour is equally important. To help you crack GDs efficiently, Attitude matterZ has a dedicated GD Module – Live sessions plus the A2Z GD handbook covering 50+ topics and their approach.

The objective of recruiter in Group Discussion is rejection of candidates- there are 10 candidates in a group and from one group, the panellist will be only selecting top 3 candidates for the interview round. To sum up, the first, second and third stages of hiring process has "REJECTION" as its sole objective and assists the recruiter in finding out the cream candidates.

Group Discussion (GD)

In the group discussion, a formal seating arrangement imitating a conference room is set up. A total of 7 to 8 are made to sit and a topic for discussion is given by the interviewer to the panel for the next 7-10 minutes. Depending on the approaches, team behaviour, thought process, communication skills and team handling skills, 2 or 3 participants are selected for the interview round. The topic of group discussion could be from static GK, current affairs, case studies, a debatable topic or even an abstract topic like 'Red or Blue'. There are different strategies to tackle each of these GD types which we will cover in detail in the GD Module.

The Personal Interview:

This is the final step in any kind of selection be it for college placements or any job in this world. These days for getting admission into many colleges personal interview becomes the most important thing, for eg., if you are giving UPSC exam, out of the 7000 rank scorers in written, ~ 700 candidates finally gets selected in the interview indicating that 1 in every 10 student will be selected even if their knowledge levels are similar. Let us understand from another example- even if you have done excellent in your CAT examination and got a 99%ile but if you are nervous and did not perform well in the interview for IIM Ahmedabad or IIM Bangalore, you will NOT be selected.

Most of the class toppers think that because they are good in studies, they will pass the interviews easily- but it doesn't happen that way! If you couldn't showcase the right skills to the interviewer sitting right in front of you, you will not get the offer. Please note that there can be one or multiple rounds in an interview (Behavioural and technical). As an aspirant, you must know how to tackle and answer each of these question types.

Personal Interview (PI)

Before answering just pause and think "Why has the interviewer asked me this question in the first place?" If you decode the WHY, half the job is done.

The objective of personal interview is SELECTION unlike the first three stages where the objective was rejection. This is because the interviewer and his team has already invested a lot of time in you in understanding who you are as a person and judging your technical skills. Understand that the interviewer is an employee himself- his KRA is to hire 2-3 students from the college. So be confident and just nail the interview with our insider tips and tricks!

GO WIN YOUR GAME!

CHAPTER FOUR

Medium of Personal Interview

Let us cover the third topic to understand- *How a Personal Interview is conducted?* Now-a-days we have 3 broad mediums for conducting a personal interview of the potential candidates namely:

- The most conventional and effective one- **Face-to Face interview** in physical (or offline) setting
- The recent one gaining momentum- (esp. in interviews with multiple rounds) via **Video Meet** (or online)
- The **Telephonic Interview-** usually taken as a first round Interview Assessment.

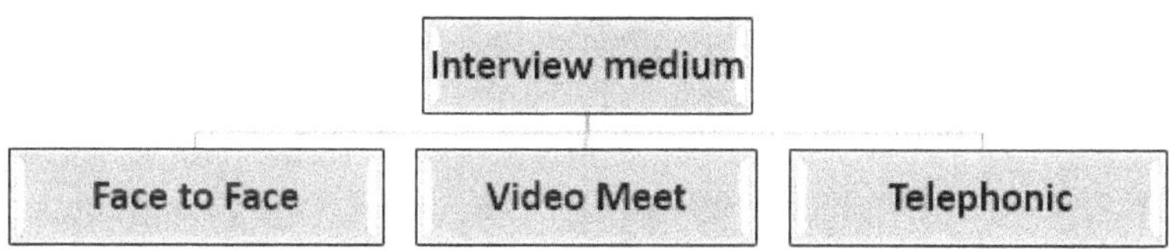

Interview Medium

Each of the above interview types needs a different preparation strategy and has its own significance as well as pros and cons. Let us understand the significance of each of them separately.

**Face-to Face interview** _in physical (or offline setting)_

Though conventional, this is still the most effective method to assess the candidate's knowledge, soft skills and most importantly- body language. Imagine a physical setting like an office desk or table where on one side there is the interviewer who would take your interview and on the other side it would be you (interviewee) who will be giving the interview for 15 or 30 or 45 minutes depending on the company's recruitment structure.

Face to Face (F2F) Interview

Note: In certain scenarios, there might be 2 or more interviewers conducting interview of one single candidate. These are called Panel interviews and are common for MBA entrance in IIMs, other B-Schools, UPSC, etc. Also, there can be an opposite scenario in companies such as TCS, Infosys, Wipro which opts for "Bulk interviews" or "Group Interviews" where there might be 3 or 4 candidates/ interviewees giving interviews together as per their respective turns. Although this is not a very effective method of taking interviews, but it is still prevalent for Pool Interviews where there are many candidates, and the recruiting team wants to interview each of the candidate for evaluating fitment in less time and picking up the best candidates from each panel.

The law of selection criteria says- _"Your first 90 seconds with the interviewer strongly decides your interview results"._

FIRST IMPRESSION MATTERS MUCH MORE THAN YOU THINK!

Video Meet (or online interviews)

Video Meets have become very prevalent especially after the pandemic when all companies shifted to online modes of recruiting people and working from home. Video meets comes at a much lesser cost to companies- the cost of travel, lodgings, and food plus it results in huge time savings of the recruiters and hence has widely become the most prevalent choices especially for entry and mid-level management roles

Online interviews

Video meet has got its own pros and cons and you need to be prepared with the below suggestions-
BEFORE THE INTERVIEW

- Always make sure that you know the UI of the platform on which the video meet would be conducted. The common platforms are Google Meet, Zoom Meet, Cisco Webex platform, Microsoft Teams and Skype. Some companies like Amazon have their own interface. You need to check for basic audio-video settings, speakers, Mikes, access to white-boards, screen sharing options, etc. It looks very clumsy and gives a bad impression when you struggle with the basic settings during your interview.

- "Your Wi-Fi will ditch you where you need it the most." This was said to me by a BCG interviewer who took half my interview on telephone and half on video meet because of unstable internet. The key learning here is to have a backup connection.
- Check your device's audio settings once; try conducting a meeting which one of your friends to confirm whether you are too loud on mike.
- In the case you have a good wall background you may keep it, else select a formal background from the background settings just before interview. I have seen students selecting flashy backgrounds like Galaxy, beaches, warzone, etc. Kindly avoid such practices and have a formal background for e.g., a library, office space, etc.
- Join the meeting 10-15 minutes before time, check that you have a bottle of water, a notebook, pen, your pen tab, charged laptop and a socket connection nearby in a quiet room.
- Just 5 minutes before the interview, kindly text the interviewer/ recruiter from HR team that you are all set.
- Avoid giving interviews on bed, sofa or a balcony. Always use a table and chair.
- You never know when you would be asked to present a case, calculate values which requires scribbling down a lot of things in your notebook. Generally, when a question comes, students jot down solutions/ strategy/points in their notebook and then try explaining it orally to the recruiter. Think it from the interviewer's perspective- he/ she feels totally disconnected when you lower your head and write on your notebook. Here's a little trick, in case you have an iPad with an apple pencil or any other laptop with a stylus, you can start writing your solution online on a whiteboard or on MS PowerPoint- whatever suits you; in case you do not have one, you may buy a pen tab for a cost-effective solution. The idea is to show the interviewer your mental diagrams, ability to structure answers and your approach. This not only keeps the interviewer engaged but many a times the interviewer participates with your solution and improves them. LEARN THE WHITE BOARDING PRACTICE BEFORE IT BECOMES COMMON AMONGST STUDENTS!
- For males, it is advisable to put on formals, (shirt with tie and blazer if needed) well buttoned till wrist, a watch and a well- groomed hair. Apply some moisturizer and do not forget to put on your favourite perfume before the interview (feel good factor matters and boosts your

confidence). You can give the interviews in your pyjamas as long as the bottom is not visible.

- For females, it is advisable to put on your formals, (shirt/ formal top), keep your hairs neat and tidy, and wear a light makeup. Keep your make up and nail paint nude and do not use flashy colours. You should wear a watch (avoid jewellery) and your favourite perfume.

<u>DURING THE INTERVIEW:</u>

- Although video meet gives you a good face to face interaction, many times it is observed that often interviewer or the interviewee switches off the camera, which is not a very good practice. It may sometimes happen that your camera is 'ON' but the interviewer has switched off his camera. At that time, you might feel a little awkward and feel that you are talking to yourself or the screen, but you need to practice it well however awkward it may seem.
- Try and greet the interviewer first. Wish a "Good Morning" and ask "How are you doing?" Put on a smiling face and confirm with the interviewer if the audio and video settings are working well and that the interviewer can see and listen you clearly. In case there is a connection issue at his end, please inform the interviewer that you are not able to hear/see him clearly.
- Adding a smile, adding talking pointers in conversations using hand gestures, counting your fingers, giving a thumbs up, nodding your heads, giving appropriate facial expressions adds to your body language and these practices must be followed. Remember, throughout the interview the interviewer must see how enthusiastic, smiling, calm and composed you are.
- Here is a little trick for you- When you are giving the interview try looking directly at the camera instead of looking on the screen. This gives the interviewer a feeling that you are directly talking to him. When you look at the screen and talk to him, on the other side on his screen your eyes appear to be in the downward direction / looking down, so look straight into the camera. You might have observed this during video calls with friends.
- Keep youself muted when you are not speaking.
-

Telephonic Interviews

These are often considered as difficult since the candidate does not have an option to showcase his/her body language and facial expressions. Even if you structure your solution properly but if you are not able to communicate properly or make him visualise your solution, it becomes very difficult to convince him since the person can only hear (and not see) you.

Telephonic Interview

Some pointers to keep in mind before Telephonic interviews:

- Always have a quiet room with a good network connection and a backup phone.
- It is advisable to use mobile phones directly and not earphones.
- Confirm with the interviewer whether your voice is audible.
- Never record a conversation- it goes against privacy policies.
- TRICK: Have your notebook with answers written on 'Top 50 questions'. Keep these tabs open in your browser- Google search, Company's websites- About the company, products page open. Have your CV right in front of you- during telephonic interviews you have this advantage that you can see and read a lot of things- don't just read; try to sound as if you are saying your own answer. This gives the impression that you have a fluent English and good communication skills.

- Always number your solutions and explain one at a time making the interviewer visualize your proposed solution. For e.g. As of now I can think of 3 ways to solve this issue, no. 1 is... and so on.

CHAPTER FIVE

Skills assessed during interviews

Whatever being the medium of interview (telephonic, face to face or a video meet) there are three broad skills that are basically assessed by the interviewer viz:

1. Technical skills- skills needed for the job role

Let us say that you are being hired for the job profile of a Market Research Analyst and despite how good your profile or communication skill is, if you do not know basic concepts of doing primary and secondary research or qualitative and quantitative research- you will not be an ideal candidate for the profile. Similarly, if you are being hired for a finance profile and you do not have a basic knowledge of financial terms or relevant internships to showcase your interest in the field, it is very difficult for you to convince the interviewer.

2. Communication Skills- and this is NOT English!

It is a very common myth that the communication skills of a person mean fluency with which he/she speaks English. Fluency does matter but there is a high chance that even a person who has a fluent English is not able to present his/ her ideas to the listener.

Communication is the process via which we explain our views to the listener (or audience) in a manner that is totally comprehensible. For interviews, we would assess communication skills in terms of how beautifully, quickly and in a structured manner you are able to communicate your thoughts and answers to the interviewer.

Assessment of communication skills is very important for selection because tomorrow when you get hired in the company, you would collaborate and work in small teams and there if you are not able to express your problems to people/team members, they would not have the whole day to listen to you and understand your requirements. Also, let us suppose you get a client facing or a sales-based role and because your communication is not that great you are not able to convince the clients on the company's product or project- you're losing out in somewhere and no company effectively would want people who cannot speak well with the clients and get businesses onboard.

The good news is that there is a trick to effective communication skills and this art could be practiced and learned in just 10 days! At Attitude matterZ, we have a separate session on improving the communication skills. Do enrol in the upcoming webinar. Now, I shall be sharing a trick with you on -Structuring your thoughts and framing answer for interviews in the next chapter.

3. <u>Leadership Skills</u>

Third skill that is assessed by the interviewer is the "Leadership Skill". What the interviewer is looking for is-

- Do you have those leadership qualities of taking a decision?
- Quality of concluding the discussion.
- Quality of convincing a lot of people to work for the company/ your team and continuously motivating them.
- Quality of taking a lead in discussions, participating and solving problems.
- Quality of managing a team now or in near future and keep your team's individual goal aligned to the organization's goal.
- Have the courage to try once yourself and convince others on trying once before saying a NO.

All the above qualities are noted during your interviews. In huge companies like Amazon, Tata, Wipro, etc., 50% of your scores during the interview your leadership skills alone. When you would join company and have an appraisal cycle you would notice that 50% of your performance depends on your personality and leadership skills only. Hence, we must understand that companies are not looking for people who can be workers alone, but they are looking forward to people who would join in an entry level position as of now, grow in the organization and lead the teams in the near future and finally lead the company by filling one of the positions for the Company's Board members. Hence, people with broader vision makes it to the interviews very easily.

CHAPTER SIX

Interview Tips- Do's and Don'ts

While we have covered Do's and Don'ts of Video Meet and Telephonic Interview in topic 3, the do's and don'ts of Face to Face Interviews were intentionally left for this section. The topic will be dealt in three parts: BEFORE , DURING and AFTER the interview.

<u>BEFORE THE INTERVIEW:</u>

1. **Dressing for Males:** A neat and ironed shirt (preferably white or light coloured) with a dark coloured formal pant, a blazer, and a tie. Blazer can be skipped if it is summer.

    i. Shirt: The buttons need to be closed till the neck- you are not here for modelling!

   ii. Shirt: Light coloured shirt- either plain or with minimal patterns.

  iii. Shirt: Button up your sleeves as well.

   iv. Pants: Formal and preferably dark colour. Do not wear an excessive tight pant and check that the length should be till the ankle.

    v. Pants: Colour of pants and blazer should be same.

   vi. Tie: Use a medium size knot stretched to the top.

  vii. Tie: The length of the tie should be till your waist belt.

 viii. Keep a handkerchief with you.

   ix. Always wear your socks, preferably white or black (avoid colours).

    x. Polish your shoes well and avoid shiny or pointed shoes. Wear black or brown shoes only.

   xi. Put on your favourite perfume. Do not use strong smells.

  xii. Hairs should be neatly done without any spikes and no fancy or Ghajini cuts.

2. **Dressing for Females**: Females can opt for both Indian and western formals. In Indian formals, you can wear kurta or a saree whereas in western formals, you can wear shirt pants or shirt and formal skirt.

i. In case you go for Indian formals, choose formal kurtis/saree with minimal design and preferably light cotton/khadi material. Avoid prints and work as much as possible.
ii. Pair your look with a closed ballets and avoid wearing sandals. Wear a light makeup, light perfume, and keep the jewelleries to a minimum. Wear a watch and avoid bangles.
iii. In case you go for Western formals and decide to put on pants and shirts, wear a light-coloured shirt with dark pants. The colour of the blazer (skip if summer) will be same as that of pants.
iv. Wear a closed shoes with a slight heel, light make up and a light perfume.
v. Hairs should be left all open if it is manageable else you may tie a bun for a formal look. No bangs should cover the face and do not use any fancy hair accessory- you are not here for modelling.
vi. Carry a handkerchief and put on a light perfume.

3. Always carry a **small notebook**/ blank sheet of paper and a **pen.**

4. Be confident and smile while you are waiting for your turn with other potential candidates. Remember, they are scared too, and your confidence and smile would take away the confidence of your competitors.

<u>DURING THE INTERVIEW:</u>

1. Ask the permission to get into the room and to sit.
2. Get inside with a smiling and confident face.
3. Greet each interviewer separately when you enter.
4. When you sit, make sure your full feet touch the ground.
5. Keep your hands folded on your lap and take out your pen and notebook and place it on the table- Remember your body language is being watched.
6. Sit straight and look towards the interview panel; do not look down, at the clock or outside. When you look down, it shows you are nervous; when you look at the clock, it gives the impression that you want to finish the interview soon and when you look outside, it gives an indication that you are not interested- and I am sure you cannot afford to do these mistakes.
7. Use had gestures wherever possible and use a soft tone.
8. Do not point via your hands to the interviewers.
9. Show an interest in whatever the interviewer speaks.
10. Pause a bit, think and then answer.

<u>AFTER THE INTERVIEW:</u>

After the interview, one must always ask for Interview feedback from the training & Placement Coordinators or the recruiter irrespective of you getting shortlisted or not. Remember, unless you know what your areas of strengths and weaknesses are, it is very difficult for you to work upon it.

Solving Top 50 Interview Questions

Now we shall be moving to solve "50 most frequently asked questions in an Interview".

The pattern of our preparation would be very different and practical. Before answering any question, we would first understand why the question is being asked in the first place, interviewer's mindset, and the category in which the question falls. Post this we will have sample answers for the questions.

You are advised to prepare your own answers using the guidelines in a separate notebook- Trust me, it helps!

CHAPTER SEVEN

Category 1: About You

S. No.	Category	Question
1		Tell me something about yourself.
2		Describe yourself.
3		Tell me something which is not there in your resume. (Accenture)
4	About You	What is the meaning of your name? (Byju's)
5		Tell me about yourself as a professional /a friend/ a son/ or a daughter.
6		Tell me about your family. (IndiaMART)
7		What should be your 'Epitaph'? (Tata Steel)

Question 1 to 7

QUESTION 1: Tell me something about yourself.

SOLUTION:

Introductory interview starts with two types of questions. First is more common- "Tell me about yourself" and second is – "Describe yourself." there will be a slight difference in answers to both the questions. Let us start with the first one:

These types of questions are **open ended questions** where the control is in your hands to take the conversation to specific direction.

The elements that your answer should contain should describe a whole package of exactly WHO YOU ARE. It is advised to keep this part between 1.5 min-2 min. *Never exceed 2.5 min.*

- One line about your name,
- Second line about the place where you were born and brought up,
- Third could be a brief about your parents,
- Followed by these comes your educational background (if you are a fresher focus more on this part). Structure and connect the education part like a story; meaning the flow of education should be from school, connected to college (mention good grades/ if you have something unique mention it) followed by the internship or work experience and the reason why you are sitting here for interview (here reason would be in a small connect of what you have done in the past or what kind of a person you are which would be directly connected to some attributes of the job role that you are applying for). An example will make it clear-

Example: "*Thank you so much for this opportunity, Sir. My name is Raman Raghav, I am from Patna, the capital city of Bihar. I come from business family and father work as a garment's retailer. My entire education was done in Patna from Kendriya Vidyalaya post which I got interested in Physics and hence decided to do an Engineering program. I was lucky enough to get into NIT Silchar in stream of Mechanical Engineering. I worked as a Design Engineer at Tata Motors Limited for 2 years in Pune and there I understood the importance, roles and responsibilities of a manager and aspired to be one and hence doing an MBA program. Now I want to apply my learnings on how to solve real life problems and presently I am looking to join a reputed organisation such as yours. Is there anything specific that you want me to add to it?*"

The above answer is suitable for final year MBA students or recent pass-outs. Certain modifications can be made for undergraduate students, wherein internship experiences can be introduced in place of work experience.

QUESTION 2: *Describe yourself.*

SOLUTION:

Now we will understand the second type: Describe yourself. This one is also **open ended, and candidate driven.**

In such type of questions, you should focus on exactly WHAT KIND OF A PERSON YOU ARE? Remember the top two or three things that makes

YOU. It is advised that one should not add about family or education too much.

One such good answer for an extrovert person who is good at networking skills and talking to people can be-

"So, if you ask about me, I am an extrovert person who likes to approach, talk and discuss any event/ topic with different people and share ideas, values and viewpoints. I believe everyone has some good and some learning experiences and when I talk to them, I always get to learn and explore hidden perspectives.

I am a kind of person who believes in simple living, high thinking and helping as many people as possible. I really consider myself lucky to have studied from great Institutions like ABC and DEF and above all to have been born to amazing parents. In a way I am satisfied with what I have, and I am ready to embark my new journey and excel in my corporate career.

I love problem solving, and many of my faculties are of the opinion that I have an entrepreneurial mindset. Is there any specific trait what you want me to describe?"

About You

QUESTION 3: Tell me something which is not there in your resume. (Accenture)

SOLUTION:

It is a usual tendency to write everything that has been achieved by us in our resume. In fact, we prepare our resume so thoroughly that even if somebody asks a question from our resume at 2:30 AM, in the middle of a sleep, we would be able answer- and this is exactly how you should prepare when it comes to your resume.

Normally when an interviewer asks you this question (Tell me something beyond your resume OR is there anything else about you apart from this sheet of paper that I have in front of me), these can be the reasons:

1) he might be genuinely interested in knowing you as a person

2) he is more interested in knowing about things that you have done which doesn't need a documentation/ or maybe things about which you are passionate

3) judge how quickly you can come up with an answer which you were not expecting; how good you can handle situations suddenly.

Hence, I always suggest keeping one pointer in mind which is not there in the resume. It need not be something very fantastic and out of the box; it could be anything related to your personal life, official life, contributions towards society, etc.

"Thank you for this opportunity. Beyond what is there in my resume, I'm a good chess player and I've participated in many notable competitions like ABC and DEF." (This answer will give the impression that you are a person with strategic skills; please don't name chess if you have never played it- DO NOT LIE)

OR

"Thank You. I am glad that you want to know more about me. I am very fond of gadgets; I like to keep myself updated with news on what is new in mobile market and what new and exciting technologies are coming up." (This answer would give an impression about you to the interviewer that you also do a lot of research on new technologies, and you like to keep yourself updated: Be ready for a cross question next; for. e.g., Which technology do you think would most likely be adopted by the new smartphone world?)

OR

"I'm very fond of event planning; be it planning small events at a society level, small wedding planning or organizing events in college. I really like that event vibe and arranging everything at the right time and launch successful event." (This point will help you project an image that tomorrow when there will be any event in the company you can be a good fit to help the HR organization. The idea is to hit positive things in the subconscious mind of the interviewer and secretly telling that- Yes, I am the one who is perfect for the job/team/company)

OR

"I love planting trees; I have organised planting drives in my city when I was in school and even today, I go back and check the conditions of the saplings that had been planted. This always gives me immense satisfaction." (This answer shows you how close you are to nature, and you care for your surroundings- CSR activities of companies- REMEMBER END OF THE DAY YOU ARE SELLING YOUR SKILL SETS TO THE RECRUITERS!)

QUESTION 4: *What is the meaning of your name? (Byju's)*

SOLUTION:

This question might sound silly to you but then it is true that many around you would have no clue of what their name means. Please do this exercise not only for this interview but also for your life- I mean you should know what your name means!

I will take an example of my own name.

"My name is Farheen. It is an Arabic word which means happiness. I really feel that this name suits me because I spread positivity and happiness around me."

QUESTION 5: *Tell me about yourself as a professional /a friend/ a son/ or a daughter.*

SOLUTION:

First understand why this question is asked. This question is asked to you to check how you assess yourself and are you even aware of how others feel about you; to check how good you are in maintaining relationships be it personal or professional. Remember, tomorrow when you will be hired in the company you will always have to work in teams with people and hence your people management skills will come into picture. Besides knowing about yourself it is also important to know what others feel about you.

Notice that this question has three parts and either of the three could be asked.

• Tell me about yourself as a professional.

In case you are a fresher and have never been exposed to a professional environment you can say, *"Till date my professional environment had been my classrooms, I understand the etiquettes of belonging to a group, asking questions, listening to others, respecting their thoughts, understanding viewpoints and finally making decisions. So, as a professional, I'm doing these things as of now.*

There were times that we had clashes in our viewpoints and those got resolved when we heard perspectives and reasonings of the other side. So, I think as a professional I'm quite decent in terms of my listening and collaborating skills but yes surely, I need to learn a lot from the corporate world out there."

In case you are a fresher but have already done an internship in the past or if you hold a work experience, this question is more relevant to you. You can structure in this manner- *"In my previous roles, I've learnt how to be professional in a corporate world setting. Earlier I was too emotional for example if the manager used to praise my work or correct me when I was wrong, I used to be either too happy or too conscious respectively. Eventually I learnt that these learnings are a part of my career progression- one cannot be correct every time; and the highs and lows of my life cannot be dependent on my day-to-day work. I have learnt to keep professional and `personal life separate; have learnt to view professional achievements like rewards and recognition as a motivation pointer, and feedback as a part of learning and correction pointer.* (Here, you can illustrate via an example of how things were in your internship or your previous job/ any notable instance and then you can conclude in this manner>> *so I think as a professional, I already have a good sense of how businesses operate and how teams behave but then again learning should never stop, and I am all ready to explore. To add on quantitatively, when it comes to people's front, during my 360-degree assessment in previous company, I have been rated quite high on leadership and soft skills."*

- Tell me about yourself as a friend.

As a part of exercise, you may write this answer on your own.

- Tell me about yourself as a son or a daughter.

Never ever say that I am not a good son or daughter, because if you yourself would admit that you are not good to closest family members, how do you expect the interviewer to react? Remember, if you yourself are not clear about what you have to do in life or you are not confident about yourself then why do you think the interviewer will even select you?

Explanation of you as a son or a daughter can be- *"I feel lucky to have been born to amazing parents, (or the best parents in the world). However busy I am, I make sure to give them time, to help them out in daily work, especially in bank statements, I make sure that I do things before they even speak to me. I do things consistently and timely such as paying bills, helping with groceries, etc. Also, since nobody is perfect, there had been times that out of laziness or certain priorities (studies) I was not available, and the work was handed to some other family member."* Try and show that most of the time you were there to help, and you are evolving and trying to become better with time. This is a very personal question and most of you can modify things basis the explanation that is given to you above.

QUESTION 6: *Tell me about your family. (IndiaMART)*

SOLUTION:

Understand interviewers are not here for a marriage proposal. They just want to know a few things about your family. Let us understand why in the very first place this question is asked:

a. The interviewer wants to know family background (business, service, urban or rural background). Note that our family plays an important role in shaping who we exactly are today.

b. Another reason why the interviewer could ask this question is to see how much proud you take in being a part of a family because going forward someday somebody might ask you about your company, so at that time how proudly you will communicate about your organization to others. So, always take a lot of pride in the kind of family and the location where you born. Always show that you are very proud of your parents, how they supported you in times of distress and how they have guided you so far.

One of the good answers can be- *"I feel blessed to be born to such amazing parents who have always supported me in my life decisions. My father is a businessman in Ranchi and my mother is a homemaker; I come from a business family, and we are into real estate* (now don't show your family business too huge otherwise they would ask you a question -why don't you join your own family business? So, do not boast). *Then talk about your siblings: I have 3 siblings, and all are younger to me, and I am the one who oversees all their education-related consultations. I hold a firm stand in my family where I give my views on family matters."*

That's it! in case there is anything special about your family just use one line but please don't start explaining your Chacha Ji, Tauji, Mauasaji and others- it is not a marriage proposal.

QUESTION 7: *What should be your 'Epitaph'? (Tata Steel)*

SOLUTION:

Epitaph means- "words that are written or said about a dead person, especially words written on a stone where he/she is buried". So, write that one liner that would describe you after death. I could write it as- "FARHEEN who lived to help others realise their dreams"

CHAPTER EIGHT

Category 2: Your Personality

S. No.	Category	Question
8		What motivates you? (Goldman Sachs)
9	Your	What are you passionate about? (Google)
10	Personality	What are your biggest strengths?
11		What are your weaknesses?

Questions 8-11

Analysing your S-W-O-T

QUESTION 8: What motivates you? (Goldman Sachs)

SOLUTION:

This very small and simple question can be a game changer. Ideally, in these types of questions where floor is completely open **(open ended and candidate driven)**, you can name anything if it can be justified. But there are certain answers that gel along very well in the corporate world viz.,

"Getting good appreciation for a project work, be it school or college has always motivated me to perform better. I like it when people appreciate me and my work and then I work towards improving it further." (now here you can face a little problem where in the interviewer can cross question you that what would happen if your work is not appreciated? Be cautious beforehand and prepare something positive for it; for example, *"Yes there had been times when I prepared something/ I put in my best efforts yet people didn't like it much, which I think is okay, so what I do is I take a genuine feedback on things and ask for improvement pointers and depending on what is feasible, I take a call to improve it; but since the original question was on motivation, my answer would be- I get motivated to do even better when my work is appreciated"*).

A second answer to this question could be- *"I get motivated when I create something meaningful which helps others save some time."* You may fit in some examples to prove this point. It could be related to work made easier at school, house, college, committee, society etc.

QUESTION 9: What are you passionate about? (Google)

SOLUTION:

This question just like the previous one throws the ball in your court **(open-ended and candidate-driven)**. This gives you a very good opportunity to talk about things that are unique to you. You need not bring your academics into it. You can talk about things like reading books, painting, any instrument that you play, sports, etc. Try to show a different side of yours, something from a social and passionate angle meaning, i.e., if you like something talk about it!

Note: If you like to read books you should know what the different genres of book are, names of famous authors, etc. If it is about basketball or cricket, you should know the rules of the game first, you must know about the renowned players in the industry and always make a note of one or two personalities from your state or city who has done a good job in the sport you are talking about.

QUESTION 10: *What are your biggest strengths?*

SOLUTION

This question might seem easy, but this has an element of **trickiness hidden inside.** So, be very cautious and very well prepared for this. Do not over promise- I have seen students over promising and using very heavy, complicated words and messing up with this question- please avoid such activities and just don't bluff. I asked this same question during a mock interview to an engineering graduate, and the reply that I got was this- *"My biggest strength is that I have no weakness!"* I mean why? why do you need to answer those heavy and filmy dialogues! You are not film star Rocky of KGF- please come back to the original world.

Some of the good answers for this question can be-

1) *"My biggest strength is that I have a very positive attitude towards life. I can keep myself motivated in times of ups and downs."* (Understand when you say words like self-motivation and positive attitude -it gets recorded in subliminal (subconscious mind) of the interviewer. Also be prepared for any example in case of a cross question, so prepare something beforehand).

2) *"My biggest strength is my networking skills. I never miss an opportunity to interact with people, discuss problems and their solutions even on day-to-day matters. This has helped me to approach problems from different perspectives."* If needed you can add this - *"I like talking to people about culture, food, sports and trending topics. Reason why I consider this as my strength is, many of my friends have approached me on how I do it so easily, because they find it difficult to build rapport with others. I hope I answered your question."*

3) *"My biggest strength is my concentration power. I can really sit for hours to complete the job that I start, and I like to dive deep into it without seeing a dip in my concentration levels. This I believe is a good quality and hence I regard this as my strength."*

QUESTION 11: *What are your weaknesses?*

SOLUTION

Understand that no human is perfect; it is OKAY to have a weakness. But please don't mess up this question by saying- *"I have a weakness; I can't talk to people"* OR *"I get nervous easily"* - any job, I repeat, any job you apply for would ask you talk to people so don't show traits that goes against the job description. Don't overreact in this question as well- for example, *"I have no weakness I can do anything and everything"*- I mean again, the recruiter wants a candidate for the job, he is not dealing with film star Rocky the owner of KGF.

Please don't say things like*" I can't say NO to someone"*. Always remember, a good employee is one who very well knows when to say a NO. Tell me about your weakness, is one such question that students take on the heart and opens black box of all the weaknesses. DON'T DO IT!

Let me talk to you about girls as well.

One of my female students answered this, *"I am very emotional, and I cry when somebody scolds me"*. Please refrain from giving such answers. You must talk about your weakness very smartly, i.e., talk about one negative aspect of yours and then show what are you doing to improve. I will give you some good answers to this question.

"Hi sir, I have a habit of procrastination. I leave things to tomorrow and hence all my work gets compiled for the last minute. I understood this when I could not complete a project in time and got a back in school/college. To come out of it, I took some professional courses on time management to prioritize my timings and based on this every morning I prepare a list of some items and try achieving it. This is helping me a lot."

The next follow up questions from the interviewer could be- **"What if you have a list of things to be done in this day and all of a sudden something urgent pops up how would you accommodate that task?"** Your answer should be- *"That happens a lot of time Sir! I don't prepare a very strict schedule for myself, and always keep some empty slots in between- this was advised by my time-management mentor in the course itself, that one should not torture oneself with a cumbersome routine, and that is exactly how I can accommodate any urgent task. If increasing the task would take a lot more time than what my routine would allow, I might re-prioritise and do the most important work for the day and would try the lesser important ones tomorrow."*

Second answer could be – *"One such weakness of mine is that I spend a lot of time on YouTube stories and Instagram reels. I am tried to minimise it as much as possible, but it didn't work out initially. This was eating a lot of my time, so I just changed the nature of content that I see on these platforms. This didn't happen overnight, but these days I see a lot of productive contents such as Sports, DIY (Do-It-Yourself) videos, product reviews, etc."*

CHAPTER NINE

Category 3: Hindsight/ Leadership Skills

S. No.	Category	Question
12	Hindsight/ Leadership skills	Where do you see yourself in the next five years?
13		Where do you see yourself in the next ten years?
14		Who is your role model? Why do you admire him/ her? In what way are you similar to your role model? (Tata Power)
15		Why should I hire you? Why do you think you are a good fit for this role?
16		Have you led a team before? Also, are you a Team Player OR a Team Leader? (Byju's)

Questions 12-16

Learn- Grow- Lead

QUESTION 12: *Where do you see yourself in the next five years?*

SOLUTION

Take a minute before you answer this question. The question wants to know, what is your idea of your career trajectory? how much understanding you have about professional growth? Please talk about some feasible career trajectory here. I really pray that you grow big, conquer the world, or become the MD of a company. We all pray this for ourselves, right? But the recruiter is not here to judge your dreams; he is here to give you a job. So please say, what he wants to hear. I should help you with some decent and industry accepted answers for this.

"5 years down the line, I see myself somewhere in the middle management position, handling a team of some 10-15 people, allocating them their targets, managing their day-to-day activities, and helping my team achieve good results. I also see myself collaborating with a lot of teams and departments in the organisation and helping the senior management in taking some strategic business decisions."

Understand the reason why we answered this question in the above manner. In an experience of 5 years, one is expected to handle a team and get work done. He/she should know how many different departments a company has and how they collaborate for an organization goal.

In some cases, you can also name of profile, for example, you may say that *"I want to be a Product Manager/ I see myself as a Product Manager who is handling product life cycle. I shall try my best to make the product a successful one, doing various activities like collaborating with teams, taking customers feedback, implementing the technologies, etc."*

This question is asked to check your vision and leadership skills- how you see things in the future. If you have a feasible, growing, and aspirational plan/trajectory for your career then you can definitely have one for the company in which you will be hired.

QUESTION 13: *Where do you see yourself in the next ten years?*

SOLUTION

Now understand, that ten years is a long period. Again, reason why this question is asked is to assess your vision and leadership skills. The interviewer wants to check your knowledge on your career trajectory and how you see yourself growing in the corporate world. Frankly speaking, after the pandemic, nobody knows what they're going to do tomorrow, situations fluctuate so much, but unfortunately, we do not have a choice here and hence let's focus on the answer-

"Well 10 years is a long period! After 10 years, I see myself somewhere in the senior management position (you can name a profile here for example, General Manager, Senior Manager, Principal Engineer, Associate Vice President, etc.) handling multiple teams of size as high as 100-150 people, driving businesses, taking some strategic level discussions for company growth. On a personal front, I see myself married with a kid and I am managing both my personal and professional life."

QUESTION 14: *Who is your role model? Why do you admire him/ her? In what way are you similar to your role model? (Tata Power)*

SOLUTION:

Focus on human psychology: Just as a nation is judged by its leader, a person is also judged via his/ her role model in life. What you follow, you eventually become, and this is the logic behind this question. In these types of questions, you can go forward to name eminent leaders- it could be any freedom fighter of the past, eminent personalities like Dr. APJ Abdul Kalam, Nelson Mandela, Barack Obama, etc. or you can also name great businessmen like Mukesh Ambani, Ratan Tata, Anand Mahindra, Rakesh Jhunjhunwala, etc.

Try avoiding the name of film stars; even if you name some film star for example, Rajinikanth then do not say *"I like the way Rajinikanth fights with 100 goons in the movie"* but say, *"I admire Rajinikanth because he has grown from a bus conductor to a notable actor given his hard work, dedication and passion towards work"*. The idea is whosoever you name, you should have one line of reasoning as to why that person is your role model in life. I also suggest avoiding naming people who are present political leaders because you never know interviewer can take things in different direction and the interview can turn into a political discussion which you would never want. One sample answer to this question is-

"I really admire Dr. APJ Abdul Kalam because of his persistence right from his childhood when he used to study under the streetlights. I have started admiring him more when I heard that his machine project was rejected by the then Prime Minister of the country Smt. Indira Gandhi. Imagine, the person whose project is rejected by the Prime Minister herself would have been shattered but then he did not give up and continued with improvising. I think I am like Kalam Sir in the manner that don't give up easily; I try going back sitting and working on the same solution in a different way only to see things are working or not. I at least give good 4-5 attempts before asking for help. I really hope I become like him one day."

The moment you take in the name of a big person and say that I want to become like him, in the subconscious mind of the interviewer, positive traits about the leader and in turn about you get registered- That is the trick! 80% of our decisions are based on points registered in the sub conscious mind.

QUESTION 15: *Why should I hire you? Why do you think you are a good fit for this role?*

SOLUTION:

Note: These types of questions need thorough preparation not only from the perspective of writing the answer but also practicing it loud in front of the mirror. Remember, interview answers without confidence and a smiling face are incomplete.

For every profile you plan to sit for, prepare this answer customised for the company and profile and keep a few pointers in your mind while framing the answer. Think it from the interviewer's perspective first- he has a job opening to which he has to map the right candidate and also keep a check on how well you to fit into the culture of the company.

Frame answer accordingly and make a note-

A very good strategy to answer these questions is to pick up some elements from the job description and present to the interviewer that you were looking to work on something of that sort only. (This shows up your interest on the profile) then map those pointers very well to your skills and then come up with a conclusion that 'this' is why I think I will be a good fit for the role. You can also mix and match your values with the organisation culture or mission vision, but please don't be dramatic here.

For example, if there is an opening in sales and you are applying for it you may answer this-

"I was looking for a role that would help me in knowing the customers very closely, would involve a lot of travel so that I can visit different places and understand different market and customer preferences. The moment I read the job description, the profile demanded exactly the skills that I possess and want to build the career in. Moreover, your company is a start-up and thrives in a fast-paced environment, and because I am looking to join a place which help me learn faster, I think I am a good fit for the role and the organisation."

QUESTION 16: *Have you led a team before? Also, are you a Team Player OR a Team Leader? (Byju's)*

SOLUTION:

Understand that in a corporate setup, everybody works as a team. Even though you get absorbed as an individual contributor, you would still have to collaborate with a lot of teams and departments to get things done. Eventually as you grow up the ladder, you will have to manage your team.

To answer this question, you may cite examples from your previous work, internship, college project experience and discuss how you have either led a team or was a part of the team.

Cite examples and say that you understand the nuances of managing the team- right from relevant work delegation to target set-up, follow ups, mix of 'carrot and stick' in the process and finally achieving results. And now depending on your interest, you can elaborate on team player or a team leader as per your choice; back it up with an example.

Tip: Generally, the undergraduate students can opt for team player option while the post graduate students are advised to chose team player as an option.

CHAPTER TEN

Category 4: Your Interests/ Achievement

S. No.	Category	Question
17	Your Interests/ achievements	List your hobbies and interests. (Flipkart)
18		List all the extra-curricular activities that you have ever participated in and mention awards.
19		Explain your project/ internship that you have done so far. (Flipkart)
20		What have you done so far for the society? (ONGC)

Questions 17 to 20

Hobbies & Interests

QUESTION 17: List your hobbies and interests. (Flipkart)

SOLUTION:

Hobbies, interests, extra curriculars, social activities hold a lot of importance in your resume. If one only writes academic-related points, list of projects, internships, and work experiences he/she only shows the professional side to the recruiter but as said before, YOUR RESUME IS YOUR FIRST FACE TO THE COMPANY YOU APPLY FOR, and hence you should always show your personality beyond academics. The interviewer wants to understand you as a person and hence your profile should be a combination of your academics, technical skills, projects, hobbies, and interests; your soft skill is examined by the interviewer himself during the process.

First, never be under the pressure of talking about an exciting hobby for example, if you say that you are passionate about cricket and you do not know the names of famous players, famous matches, rules of the game (such as cricket has 42 rules) then you will land yourself into a trouble. You can name cricket, basketball, tennis etc. when it comes to sports (but be honest), you can mention cooking, gardening, singing or any other hobby you have.

If you say that you sing, depending on the mood of the interviewer be prepared with a one liner song, or with the names of some famous musicians or singers. If you mention reading books, you should know at least the top authors in the famous genres. The idea is whatever you say, you should have sound backup of things. If you do not have a specific hobby, it is completely okay to say that I watch Instagram reels during my free time or I help my mom with the household chores or I spend time with my grandparents, etc.

QUESTION 18: List all the extra-curricular activities that you have ever participated in and mention awards.

SOLUTION:

In case you are a person who has a lot of extracurricular activities mentioned on the resume such as sports, debates, elocutions, corporate competitions, etc. at school, college or even at community level, keep a list of the certificates received (participation + winning), be prepared with the names of the events where you participated, organisers and the Chief Guests who participated, for e.g. if you were the winner in a Techfest named 'Aarohan' at BIT Mesra, you should know that Aarohan is organised by Student's Chapter of BIT Mesra.

Interviewer is not here to know how good a chess player you are or how fast you can run and how many medals you have brought on the table, the question is only a means to know more about you and gauge your seriousness in other fields as well. Also, suppose that you have never won in any competition you participated in the past, in such a scenario, it is completely okay to say that you have participated in some competitions organised at school/ college level in which unfortunately you could not get Top Rank in the competition, but you enjoyed participating. It is more about enjoying than winning the game.

QUESTION 19: *Explain your projects/internships that you have done so far. (Flipkart)*

SOLUTION:

Pick up your recent or most relevant Project or Internship and use the below structure to frame answer:

- Objective: Describe the project objective in one line here.
- Impact/Importance: What was the need to solve this problem? Try quantifying the impact (or projected outcome)
- How: Planning and execution of the solution. What extra effort/ out of the box ideas were applied.
- Result: Was the problem solved? Was it a one-time short-term solution or you fixed the issue for ever? As compared to projected outcome what was the % age achievement? How was the project received in the organisation/ or by faculty.

QUESTION 20: *What have you done so far for the society? (ONGC)*

SOLUTION

This question shows your concern towards the society and what you give back to the world. This is not only important for your upcoming interviews but also for future. For students who apply for any of the university abroad (via GRE/ GMAT examinations) should make a note of the fact that a large weightage of your resume is given to your past contributions to societal work.

If you have not done anything significant as of now, my suggestion is to take an internship on teaching, fund raising, organising camps, etc. from reputed NGOs. If you can get United Nations/ WHO/ UNICEF on your CV, nothing like it. If possible, try showing your hobbies and interests a bit aligned to how good you are as a citizen of the country or as a member of the society (could be your own mohalla, society apartment building or city). In fact, if you look at the website of any mature company there would be different sections such as- About Us/ Services/Contact us followed by a one pager which talks about Corporate Social Responsibility (CSR) activities of the company and hence different elements including societal one is important in framing up the image. One good answer could be-

"I really like to contribute to organising blood donation camps. During a medical emergency of a close family member, I realised the value of timely help to the one in need and from that time I started organising a lot of blood donation camps and educate the society on helping somebody in need."

Another answer could be:

"I have a passion towards planting trees. If you ever happened to visit my society XYZ colony of XYZ city, you would find there is a green area for meditation which has been designed by me where we planted all oxygen rich trees like neem, peepal etc. We did a similar activity at my school as well where in during friendship day we started a trend of gifting saplings to each other. I know these things quite small but whenever I see the tree growing, I feel immense satisfaction that at least I was able to do something for the society and I'm sure I'm going to do much more going forward."

CHAPTER ELEVEN

Category 5: Behavioural Questions

S. No.	Category	Question
21		How do you typically respond to problems? (These problems could be in any sphere of your life)
22		Give instances where you took charge of a difficult situation and resolved it. (Amazon)
23		What was the toughest decision you had to make? OR What was the toughest challenge you had to take up and how did you go about it? (Google)
24	Behavioural questions	Describe one incident or event where you initially stumbled, but eventually recovered and were able to achieve your objectives. (Amazon)
25		Imagine a situation that you have a priority task lined up. How will you accommodate the task given that you already have list of tasks lined up for the day? (Directi)
26		What would you do if you are not selected?(Yes Bank)
27		What is your plan B if you don't get selected in the entire campus placements? (HUL)

Questions 21 to 27

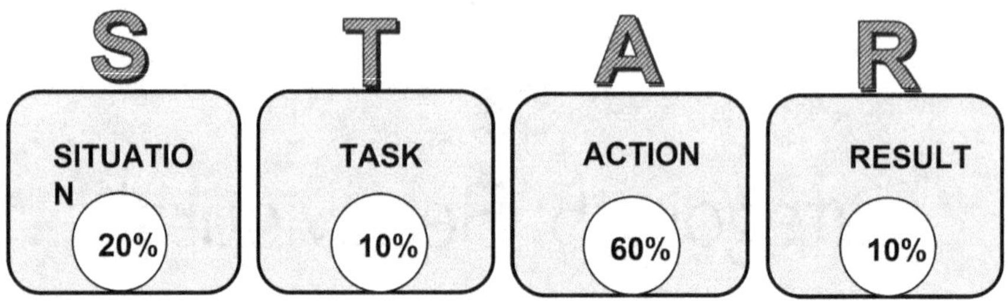

Answering Technique

QUESTION 21. How do you typically respond to problems? (These problems could be in any sphere of your life)

SOLUTION:

"When things go wrong or I have a problem at hand, first thing I do is to take a pen and a paper and try to write down situation, the actual problem, etc. Psychology says that when you say something when you're confused, you tend to make trivial matters bigger, so it is generally advisable to document crisp pointers to work upon. So, this is my formula of facing the problem and separating symptoms from actual problems. Secondly, I breakdown the problems into parts let's say number 1 number 2 number 3 and thirdly prioritise on which work should I do first. So far, I have been getting my answers using this logic. I also understand that we cannot solve our 100% problems and hence there is a need to prioritise. I hope I answered your question."

QUESTION 22. Give instances where you took charge of a difficult situation and resolved it. (Amazon)

SOLUTION:

This question is asked to check how you typically behave when you are put into a difficult situation. It is to be noted that a person's behaviour in a normal circumstance and that during handling a critical problem drastically differs. A lot of interviewers want to check how do you deal with problems because problem solving is a crucial a part of corporate life. Try to remember one difficult situation of your life (and do not fake it) and list down how have you resolved it- Use the below structure:

- Situation: Describe the situation in one or two lines here.
- Impact/Importance: Why do you need to solve this problem?
- How: Planning and execution of the solution. What extra effort/ out of the box ideas were applied.
- Result: Was the problem solved? Was it a one-time short-term solution or you fixed the issue for ever?

QUESTION 23. *What was the toughest decision you had to make? OR What was the toughest challenge you had to take up and how did you go about it? (Google)*

SOLUTION

Here you are free to talk about any tough decision that had been taken in the past. It could be from your personal or professional life (**open ended and candidate driven**). However, it is advised that being in the professional field, one must discuss about decisions that have shaped his/her career so far.

One of the good answers could be your decision to join the present B. Tech or MBA college that you are into. During your admission phase you had 5 to 6 college options for admission. The decision was very crucial since it was a matter of your career progression. Then based on information available, you had 4-5 different parameters to evaluate the choices and finally you decided to take the admission in the present college. The top 4-5 parameters could be the faculty and publications record, the branch or specialization that the college is offering, location of the college, past records in terms of placements, reviews for seniors, etc.

You may frame your customised answer keeping the above points in mind.

QUESTION 24: Describe one incident or event where you initially stumbled, but eventually recovered and were able to achieve your objectives. (Amazon)

SOLUTION:

This question is **open-ended and candidate-driven,** and like previous question, it is advisable to cite examples from professional life. Think of a scenario, when you planned an approach to the problem but when you were faced with the challenge of execution, there was a huge mismatch and then you eventually re-planned and reworked to set things right.

One example could be: *"During my market research internship at GSK, I was asked to collect feedback of 10 distributors and 10 doctors dealing with women heath products and Ayurveda. This was going to be my first field exposure and since I had never been exposed to the actual market earlier, I was confident that I would be greeted well and within a span of 5 days I would cover all the targeted distributors and doctors and accordingly, I prepared my route-plan for coverage. However, upon travelling the wholesale markets, locating distributors, asking/requesting, and even begging for some time from both clients and distributors, I realised how tricky the job was. In 5 days, upon trying 11 clients, I could collect feedback of only 2. Then I understood the importance of feasible planning and better execution. So, upon talking to a few seniors, I re-strategized my route plan, called for appointments before visit and instead of directly approaching for survey form, this time I had a better pitch where some statistics on the industry benchmarks and some suggestions to soothe the distributors' pain-points were also added. With this strategy, I was able to complete 18 more clients in the next 8 days."*

QUESTION 25: Imagine a situation that you have a priority task lined up. How will you accommodate the task given that you already have list of tasks lined up for the day? (Directi)

SOLUTION:

These are situational questions where the candidate is given a hypothetical scenario to work upon and explain his/her course of action in case such a situation arises. This question is more relevant for people with work or internship experience.

You may say that given your corporate experience you know that such types of scenarios are very common. Everybody who works in an organization has his own task list for the day but many a times any priority task can come up given the business requirements. If such a scenario arises in future, I would re-prioritise my entire day and try accommodating the priority task first followed by the lesser priority ones. I would obviously try to complete the entire work on time but if in case any of my usual routine work gets delayed then that shall be completed either by end of the day or by next morning. In fact managers should align the work of the team members in such a manner that people always have some slots where in emergency/ priority task can be accomodated.

QUESTION 26: *What would you do if you are not selected?(Yes Bank)*

SOLUTION:

Always pause for 2 seconds before answering this question.

The interviewer wants to see your reaction when he kills your motivation, attacks on the most vulnerable side of yours. During the corporate career, many things can go unplanned and many-a times we would fail as well, but what is important is how would you recover it and how do you re-plan and re-execute when things fall apart.

One good answer is, *"Sir, I really want to be selected and be a part Nestle (Company name). However, if I do not get through, I shall try for the same role/profile of a Sales Manager at FMCG companies such as Britannia or HUL. But given a preference, I would choose Nestle over all because I have heard very positive reviews on work culture and employee satisfaction from my seniors- so much, that I really want to join your organisation and experience the same journey".*

QUESTION 27: *What is your plan B if you don't get selected in the entire campus placements? (HUL)*

SOLUTION:

Again, pause for 2 seconds, show a serious face, and then begin, *"I am confident that I shall secure a placement given my knowledge, preparation and motivation, but let us say if we have a hypothetical scenario where I did not get placed in the campus, I think I would start applying for pool hiring and off campus rounds, but this time with a difference. Before applying, I shall sit with the feedbacks provided to me by the T&P committee, interviewers, friends, etc. and work on my mistakes."*

This answer would show how well you understand self-realisation and self-assessment and how even if things go wrong, you still have the courage to work harder and fight.

CHAPTER TWELVE

Category 6: Negative Questions

S. No.	Category	Question
28		Why do you have such poor grades/ academic performance? (BCG)
29	Negative questions	What you do not like about this college? (Wipro)
30		What you did not like about our company?
31		Where do you think is the present Govt is lacking? What would you have done different if you were in that position? (TAS)

Questions 28-31

Negative questions

QUESTION 28: Why do you have such poor grades/ academic performance? (BCG)

SOLUTION

Before answering this question, first analyse your academic records carefully.

- If your 10th, 12th, Graduation %ages is between 60-80 then, do not admit that you have poor grades/ academic performance. Show how good you are in extra curriculars, solving real life problems via implementing the learnt concepts. You may say that maybe you are not that great in memorizing a lot of things, but your concepts are clear, and you have average grades.
- If your 10th, 12th, Graduation %ages is below 60% then you are in a bit trouble. Convey that you are not a very good memoriser but instead you can solve the practical problems. Here you can also say that not everyone in class is good in academics and there are extra curriculars as well that defines you as a person. For example, if you are applying for the profile of Relationship Manager or Sales Manager, your networking skills, real life problem-solving and people management would matter more than your memorising skills or grades. Try using these pointers for preparing your own answer

QUESTION 29: What you do not like about this college? (Wipro)

SOLUTION

Understand why this question is asked. The question is negative, and the interviewer wants to now hear how complaining you can become if things are not as per your expectations. In corporates many-a-times it happens that due to business requirements you might have additional working hours, working weekends, sudden project, team, or location change- at that point in time it might become difficult for you to adjust. On one hand there will always be employees in an organisation who complains and spreads negativity but on the other hand there would be employees who view these not as burden but as opportunity to prove themselves; and the interviewer wants to understand you belong to which category.

One good answer to this question can be, *"Talking about practical life, nothing is perfect; in fact, things are very subjective- I may rate a product "excellent" whereas you might rate it only as "average". There are a few things that I do not like about the college such as the mess food and the insufficient lab-equipment because of which sometimes are practical gets hampered. But there is a positive aspect too; once some of us complained, actions have been taken to make the situation better and as students, we should also understand that things do not change overnight. These were the two things that I could remember but then these are manageable, and I believe every college will have something negative or the other."*

Try showing you are a flexible person who sees positive side of the story and does not fuss about any ongoing ups and downs- every company wants self-motivated and positive employees.

QUESTION 30: *What you did not like about our company?*

SOLUTION

The reason why this question is asked is the same as previous one.

- You may discuss about any element or any round in the hiring process which you didn't like much, but you should be also ready for cross questions and <u>with an alternative solution</u>. Do not use a critical tone, instead, use a suggestive tone.
- You may discuss about an element/content/strategy from the website or social media pages which you didn't like and make sure that you <u>have an alternative solution</u>.

QUESTION 31: *Where do you think is the present Govt is lacking? What would you have done different if you were in*

that position? (TAS)

SOLUTION

Readers are strictly advised to not take the names of any political leaders, news anchors or even the Prime Minister. The address should always be made as "The Government of India/ the then Government of India" and so on. Never name any political party for good or bad decisions, ruling, etc. Even if you are a string follower of any party, keep your ideologies outside the interview room.

In such scenarios, the interviewer can name any Current affair topic of static GK Topics (like demonetisation, GST, lockdown, farmer's bill, CAA, etc). You are advised to read and study about current affairs and some of the past Government reforms and keep yourself updated. Once you find the loopholes in any of Government reforms, find alternative solution and explain it to the interviewer. Do not say in a criticising tone. Whenever you are approaching on questions of static GK or history, do not be opinionated and follow a balanced approach.

Category 7: Your preparedness

S. No.	Category	Question
32		Have you gone through our (company's) website? What do you know about this company? (Emami)
33		What do you know about this Industry? (HUL)
34		What do you know about the Job Description?
35		Why do you want to join our company?
36	Your Preparedness	Why do you want to join this role? OR is this role aligned to your career objectives? Please explain how?
37		Why did you choose to do MBA?
38		How do you plan to learn this skill (could be a software/ digital marketing/ coding,etc) since you do not know about it? (Disney)
39		Why should I hire you and not others? (McKinsey)

Questions 32 to 39

QUESTION 32: *Have you gone through our (company's) website? What do you know about this company? (Emami)*

SOLUTION

This question is asked to gauge your seriousness towards the company you are applying for. Always make sure you study and research about the company before you sit for the interview.

In case your college has a placement week like most IIMs, try and prepare about every company before-hand.

Open Wikipedia and company's home page; prepare a one-pager about the company in the below format-

- Company name/ Year of Establishment/ Headquarters/ branches/ employees
- Brief History/nature of business/ Vision/Mission
- Famous brands/ Business units/ verticals
- Latest news/ CSR activities/ Any notable pointer about the company
- If possible, do a SWOT (Strength/Weakness/Opportunity/Threats) and a PESTLE (Political/Economic/Social/Technological/Legal/ Environmental)

QUESTION 33: *What do you know about this Industry? (HUL)*

SOLUTION

This question is asked to understand how well-versed you are with the macro-economic factors that is guiding the industry. Many pointers for this would come from the previous question where the industry would be covered in the SWOT and PESTLE analysis of the company. It is advisable to prepare following points:

1. Industry size in India and World and its CAGR
2. Top 3 players in the market (Market Share analysis)

3. Position of the company in the industry
4. Any recent news that might have impacted the business.

QUESTION 34: *What do you know about the Job Description?*

SOLUTION

It is advisable to study well about the profile you are applying for; you may follow the below 3 stage approach for the same:

- You must read all fields including location, job title, eligibility, list of important keywords in the job description and software/ certifications/ skills needed for the job.
- Research on the profile on Google/ YouTube. For example, if you are applying for the profile of an area manager at Tata Motors, you may type in "A typical day in the life of Tata Motors' Sales Team" on popular search engines.
- Try connecting with your college senior in the same profile OR reach out to people with similar profiles on LinkedIn.

QUESTION 35: *Why do you want to join our company?*

SOLUTION

To answer this question, start with what all research you have done about the company followed by the job profile and then talking about the employee satisfaction levels (if possible, share an example of your senior's review here)

"Sir, the reason why I want to join Tata Motors is because it is the largest automotive player in Asia, hence I will have a chance to learn from the best. I was looking for a role in strategy and you are offering me exactly the same profile. I also did some research on quality of work and work life balance of Tata Motors on Glassdoor, and it was rated 4.8/5.0 (>200 ratings) plus my senior,

Mr. Harshad Mehta too praised a lot about the learning culture. These are the reasons why I really desire to be a part of your organisation."

QUESTION 36: *Why do you want to join this role? OR is this role aligned to your career objectives? Please explain how?*

SOLUTION

Align your specialisation and favourite subjects to the role and answer that you really wanted to work in this specialisation area. As a part of your role- research activity, you must check the career trajectory/ designations that this role can offer you.

Picking up points from the two above, you can frame your customised answer.

QUESTION 37: *Why did you choose to do MBA?*

SOLUTION

Everybody has their own reason to join a B-School/ Engineering or medical. Never say that somebody in the family or friend suggested and therefore you joined the program. Your answer should be logical, and it should be a result of interest or realisation. One of the answers can be-

"When I was in my previous company, I really liked the way my manager handled the entire team right for example, correct work delegation, follow-ups, maintaining a balance of motivation and strictness, resolving people issues in team, etc. While we focussed on our day-to-day tasks, he focussed on ensuring that our day-to-day tasks are aligned to team and in turn business goals. I was very much inspired by his style of working and I noticed that most managers in the company does the same job in their own styles. I decided to do an MBA and wanted to analyse things from a broader perspective. Moreover, I wanted to spend 2 years and enjoy the journey as well".

QUESTION 38: *How do you plan to learn this skill (could be a software/ digital marketing/ coding,etc) since you do not know about it? (Disney)*

SOLUTION

Let us suppose that you are being interviewed for a role in Email Marketing. For this, you should know a platform for email automation (for example, Mailchimp/ Sen grid, etc.), advance excel and Google app scripts. Let us assume you do not know about any of these skills. In such a scenario, you may answer giving the reference of publicly available courses on YouTube or other good platforms, books, paid courses, etc. saying that you shall learn the skills in the next 10-15 days by making use of the courses available in the market and since you are a quick learner, you would get to understand the concepts and their application first.

<u>**Note:**</u> Do not shy away from asking the interviewer if he can suggest some good resources.

Now, having done these, you may say that from your internship or work experience, you are aware that the practical learning comes via the job role itself, but it is always good once you have sound back-ups of the concepts.

QUESTION 39: *Why should I hire you and not others? (McKinsey)*

SOLUTION

These types of questions are generally asked somewhere towards the end of the interview. Questions can be: Why should we hire you? What is so unique about you? Why should I hire you and not others?

There is a thumb rule to answer these types of questions. You are ideally selling your skill sets over your competitors. Thumb rule of sales advise you to never talk negative about competitor's product but instead talk about how your product/service can solve the customer's issue. You should basically talk about your strength areas that relates to the job requirement. For example, if it is a sales-based job, you can talk about your negotiating skills, you can say that you are a team player and a travel-lover. Remember, this question is a trap- never ever talk anything negative about other participants and do not try to show yourself better than others; just try to show yourself good.

So, one of the possible answers of 'Why should I hire you and not others' can be- *"Sir I cannot talk about others on how well they qualify for this job opportunity, but I definitely know about myself and both my short and long-term interest is perfectly aligned to your organisation's values/ mission. I understand that I might not know some of the technical skills as of now, but I am very enthusiastic and keen on learning. Also, the reason why I am applying for this position is that I want to make a career in XYZ profile (name the job profile for which you are giving interview/ some related job profile). So, given my present skill sets, my career interests and most importantly my positive attitude towards learning are the reasons why I think I am really a good fit in this role."*

CHAPTER FOURTEEN

Category 8: All time favourite questions

S. No.	Category	Question
40		What is consulting? (Deloitte)
41		Why do you think are consultants paid so high?(BCG)
42		What is the difference between marketing and sales?
43		What is the daily revenue of Business Standard?
44	All time favourite questions	Marketing plan: Share me a plan to sell 100 units of baby food online. (Moglix)
45		Your Client is the owner of automobile dealership in Delhi and is expecting flat sales. Find reasons and give recommendations. (Bain & Co.)
46		How will you rate yourself as a 1) planner 2) executioner?
47		What is MBA in Operations?
48		How important do you think is digital marketing for our business?
49		Do you have any questions to ask me?
50		What is your salary expectation?

Questions 40 to 50

QUESTION 40: What is consulting? (Deloitte)

SOLUTION

According to Deloitte, *"Consulting is the process of helping clients solve their most pressing business problems or issues."* For simplicity, you might take the analogue of a doctor and a patient; the doctor being consultant and the patient being the client/ customer/ company.

A patient observing signs of illness and need for treatment walks up to the doctor for consultation on cure. The doctor who has years of experience in dealing with similar illness for number of patients, understands the symptoms and underlying illness after doing certain tests. Post this, a consultation fee is charged, and certain medications are prescribed.

Apply the same scenario to the consulting world as well. Here the companies/ clients/ customers walk up to the consultants for issues related to their business; it could be with strategy, revenue, profits, market entry, etc. Now, consultants have years of experience in dealing with similar companies and similar issues. Basis some research and questions, he would then help the clients with expert advice, pilot runs or maybe executions.

If you understand the above example well, you can very confidently tackle primary level questions on consulting.

QUESTION 41: Why do you think are consultants paid so high?(BCG)

SOLUTION

In this question, one can focus on the importance of getting right diagnosis at the right time. Just as the medical aid delay can be a threat, delay in correction pointers for businesses in their life cycle can cause havoc. Organisations might experience financial losses, attrition, loss of company's vision and execution challenges. Right consultation is crucial to prevent this disaster, and we know in this business world that everything comes at a price; more the value more is the price.

According to Harvard Business Review, below are consulting's eight fundamental objectives, arranged hierarchically:

1. Providing information to a client
2. Solving a client's problems
3. Making a diagnosis, which may necessitate redefinition of the problem
4. Making recommendations based on the diagnosis
5. Assisting with implementation of recommended solutions
6. Building a consensus and commitment around corrective action
7. Facilitating client learning—that is, teaching clients how to resolve similar problems in the future
8. Permanently improving organizational effectiveness

QUESTION 42: *What is the difference between marketing and sales?*

SOLUTION

Marketing is about building brand awareness and creating a positive image and viewership; and sales turn that viewership into revenues and profits by making the end customers finally pay the price. Marketing and sales go hand in hand- while Marketing is about creating a PULL or demand in the market about the product/service, sales ensures that enough PUSH is maintained, and the goods are finally sold to the end customers. The process of sales involves a combination of planning and execution, ensuring that right products are available at the right time to right customers. The market feedback is then transferred to the marketing team which accordingly works on the product, target audience, communication pointers, etc.

In case the interviewer asks a cross-question and asks *"What do you think is more important? Sales Or Marketing?"* you may say this- *"Sir, in my opinion like I said before Marketing and Sales go hand in hand, both are equally important. A perfect balance of pull and push needs to be maintained for achieving the goal of revenue. But depending on the nature of business, products, industry, and the vintage of the brand in the market, marketing and sales can have difference in budget split, workforce, man-hours, etc. But one cannot ignore either of the two."*

QUESTION 43: *What is the daily revenue of Business Standard?*

SOLUTION

In the above question, the interviewer is not looking at a fixed number as an answer, rather he is looking at your approach to arrive at the number. These types of questions are called **'guesstimates'** where the interviewer expects you to make a realistic guess and estimate the results. Some more examples could be- What is the total number of trees in your college? How many packets of breads are consumed in your mess each day? etc. For such type of questions, you may visit our website www.attitudematterz.com and book a guesstimate session or buy our A2Z Handbook on Guesstimates.

Now, Business Standard, being a newspaper can have 2 direct sources of revenue- Subscription charges (price of newspaper) and the ads that appear on the pages. Besides, this since the world is moving towards digital, we will also have revenues from online subscriptions and ads.

Assumptions:

- One newspaper is bought in 1 house
- Business standard is distributed in Urban families
- Online revenue is 20% of offline revenue
- Commercial copies is 50% of Domestic Copy
- Print ads are charged only on per ad basis

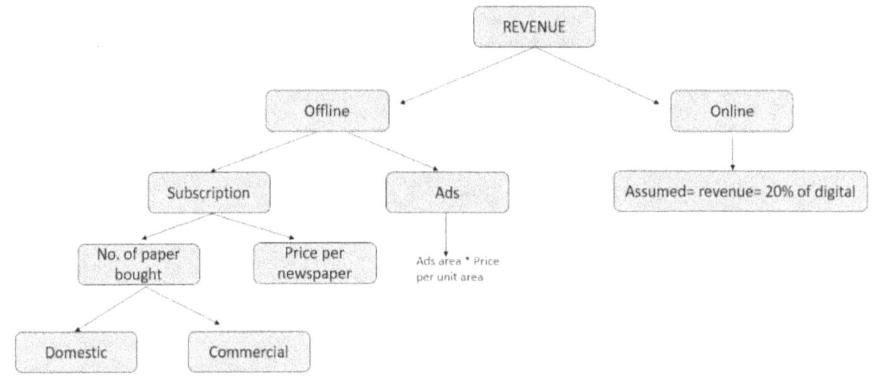

Calculation approach

Step 1: Calculate domestic revenue:

- Population of India=120 Crores
- Assuming 5 people in a family, number of households= 120/5= 24 Crores.
- Urban families= 30% of 24 Crores= 7.2 Crores
- English newspaper penetration=25% of 7.2 Crores= 1.8 Crores
- Considering Market Share of Business Standard (10%), daily household where Business Standard sell= 10% *1.8 Crores= 18 Lakh
- Considering price of newspaper as Rs. 10/copy, daily domestic revenue= 18 Lakh*10=180 Lakh

Step 2: Calculate commercial revenue:

- Commercial copy= 50% of domestic= 50% of 18 lakh= 9 lakh
- Commercial revenue= 9 lakh*10= 90 Lakh

Total Offline subscription revenue= 180 Lakh+ 90 Lakh= 270 Lakh daily
Step 3: Calculating Ads revenue

- Assume = No. of pages in newspaper= 18 and per page there are 3 ads of equal sizes: Total ads = 18*3=54 per newspaper

- Assuming price of 1 ad = 2 lakh; the total ad revenue= 54*2=108 Lakh

Total Offline business revenue= Subscription+ Ads = 270 Lakhs+108 Lakhs= <u>378 (~380)Lakh</u> daily.

Step 4: Calculating Online revenue

As per the assumption, online revenue is 20% of offline revenue, hence,

Online revenue= 20% * 380 Lakh=76 Lakh

Hence, TOTAL BUSINESS STANDARD DAILY REVENUE= ONLINE + OFFLINE

76+ 380 =456 LAKH

~4.5 CRORES DAILY

For more such questions, with detailed explanation, you may visit our website www.attitudematterz.com and book a guesstimate session or buy our A2Z Handbook on Guesstimates.

QUESTION 44: *Marketing plan: Share me a plan to sell 100 units of baby food online. (Moglix)*

SOLUTION

We shall approach this question only by estimating via our digital marketing plan

Suppose the baby food is available on the company's website only and we need to sell it via ads. Since the baby food already has a market which buys on its own, using the pareto principle we deduce that 20% of the sales happen via its regular Target Group and rest 80% happens via our ads.

So now, our task is to sell 80 units via ads.

Let us say, we decide to run a YouTube skippable ad and do a placement targeting of our ads on channels with parenting content. To sell 80 units, we need to get 20,000 ad impression to finally make a purchase.

After discussing these numbers, you might want to say that after ad optimisation, instead of 20,000 impressions, sales can happen with 12000 impressions, given that YouTube algorithm will now be able to target precise customers.

Now the interviewer can have a follow up question on ads cost, revenue, and profits; for this, you shall need some detailed figures. But remember, your plan should have impressions(views), clicks and sale followed by a choice of platform (YouTube) and a choice of ad (skippable ad).

Digital Marketing Funnel

QUESTION 45: Your Client is the owner of automobile dealership in Delhi and is expecting flat sales. Find reasons and give recommendations. (Bain & Co.)

SOLUTION

These types of questions are a part of case interviews where the candidate is given a real-life scenario to inspect, find out the actual reason and finally come up with certain recommendations. Such questions require heavy practice. For more such questions, with detailed explanation, you may visit our website www.attitudematterz.com and book a consulting session or buy our A2Z Handbook on consulting case preparation.

I= Interviewer

C=Candidate

C=> So, our client is the owner of an automobile dealership in Delhi and is expecting flat sales. I have to find out the reasons for the same and give recommendations. Am I correct?

I=> Yes, go on!

C=> Before jumping into solution, I needed to ask you certain clarifying questions.

I=> Okay.

C=> I wanted to understand the segment of automobile dealership, size of dealership and revenue streams of client?

I=> The client is a commercial Tata Truck dealer in Delhi with close to 50 units being sold per month. The revenue streams are from sale of vehicles as well as from servicing.

C=> Since the client is facing flat sales, I wanted to understand since how long this problem is experienced and the hit in sales is in number of vehicles or service units. Also, are other similar dealerships of Tata in Delhi struggling with same issues?

I=> This problem is being experienced since last 1.5 years and the number of service units have taken a hit. Sales numbers does not show any major change.

To answer your second question, the other similar dealers are doing fine.

C=> Thank You Sir! That is a great lead. So, the problem is not external; since the vehicle sales number is similar, it is not the marketing, BTL, product related issue.

I can now visualise that the problem seems to be internal towards service. Can you please help me in understanding that if servicing revenue is an issue, what has changed, the number of customers has gone down(demand) or our client's manpower count/ quality (supply) has gone down?

I=> The number of customers has taken a major hit.

C=> The number of customers visiting is directly proportional to the customer experience factor. Since it is a commercial truck, I assume major factors in servicing would be TAT, cost of servicing, location, operational hours of showroom, quality of servicing. Do we have any measurement of these factors?

I=> Well, the TAT of vehicle servicing has increased from an average of 2.4 days in 2019 to 3.9 days now in 2022. During covid, the old workers were sacked, and the team now has hired fresh mechanics.

C=> Thank You Sir! Since these are commercial trucks, delay in each day causes loss in revenue for the customers. The reason is not the quantity of manpower but with the quality of manpower.

My recommendations are to hire an expert trainer as an immediate resolution and train the team in doing work faster. To drive initially, KRA on TAT of servicing should be a part of every employee's incentive structure including the general manager. The client needs to review TAT of servicing and should use the 2019 figures as a benchmark.

I=> Yes! The recommendations sound good!

QUESTION 46: *How will you rate yourself as a 1) planner executioner?*

SOLUTION

Many a times the interviewer ask questions related to self-assessment and might give you an assessment parameter and ask you to rate yourself; for example, in the above question you are asked to rate yourself as a planner or an executioner.

In these types of questions, it is better to rate yourself on a scale of 10. Also, never rate yourself below 7 because if do so, it simply indicates that you yourself admit that you are not amongst the potential candidates. It is always advised to rate yourself somewhere between 7.5 to 8 and then add to the interviewer that once you will have a good experience of actual job-based scenarios, you know for sure that you will improve a lot and those extra 2 pointers would then be added.

QUESTION 47: *What is MBA in Operations?*

SOLUTION

An MBA in operations management is responsible for designing the company's processes and ensuring that they are efficient and effective. Operations ensure that all the corporate planning gets executed timely on ground.

The tasks in operations will comprise of planning, organizing, supervising, and ensuring that actuals are in line with the plannings.

QUESTION 48: How important do you think is digital marketing for our business?

SOLUTION

During pandemic, every company realised the importance of an having an online presence. Even Starbucks started selling coffee online and this is the main reason why you would see questions on digital marketing in many interviews these days. Understand, different companies can have different ways of making an online presence, some sell via google ads, some via FB/ Instagram and some via IndiaMART/ Justdial. What is important for you is to show the interviewer some relevant statistics on digital marketing viz.,

i. US has spent 51% of its ad revenue on digital marketing Vs 49% in Traditional marketing in 2021 and India will follow the trend.

ii. Facebook users have been growing ever since its inception and India has highest number of Instagram users in the world. Thus, indicating that the target group is shifting online and hence there is a need to realign our marketing strategies to these changing trends.

Now frame your answer using the above pointers and add the industry benchmarks and industry best practices. You are advised to glance through company's and its top competitor's digital assets- website and social media pages.

QUESTION 49: Do you have any questions to ask me?

SOLUTION

This question is generally asked during the completion of the interview. By the time this question arrives, the interviewee already has an idea on how well the interview was. It is strongly advised not to discuss on salary and location during this moment. One of the common mistake sales candidates do at this stage is, they ask, "After how much time can I expect a profile change into marketing?"- This question instantly gives the impression that you are not interested in sales, and you can switch to marketing if given a chance; so kindly be careful and refrain asking these in the interview round. These questions can be asked by HR or recruiter later.

You can ask any of the below mentioned question:

- Thank You for the opportunity! I wanted to understand how does a typical day of ABC (Profile) in your company looks like?
- Thank You for the opportunity! I wanted to understand the career trajectory if I am hired for the position.
- What is the best part about working at DEF (Name the company)?

What are the new tools/software/skills that this job requires which one should start preparing immediately.

QUESTION 50: *What is your salary expectation?*

SOLUTION

This is the most important question not because it is about money but because many working professionals also makes a lot of mistakes here. I will answer this question in two parts: the first part for freshers and the second part for working professionals.

<u>**FRESHERS:**</u> There are two types of job roles, first is the on campus hiring and second one is off campus. Luckily, during the **on campus hiring**, Training & Placement coordinators have already done the CTC job for us, and the final offer is attached to the package, so you there is no need to talk about salary during campus hiring.

The second scenario is when you apply your luck in the **off campus hiring**, and since you are a fresher with no experience this is how you should answer this question, *"I have no work experience but in my college the average placement package is around xx LPA(please increase this amount by 15-20%), so being a fresher this is what would be my minimum expectations from the company that will be joining."*

Under normal circumstances what happens is when you quote a value the recruiter tries to negotiate you for something around 15 to 20% lower than what has been quoted, hence, it is always advised to quote an amount somewhat higher than the average college placement report. For example, if your college placement is around 5 LPA you can say is around 6 LPA.

Another strategy to solve this type of question is you might say that for a similar profile and for a similar company as yours this was the salary range in my college, so this is my minimum expectation from your company as well.

<u>WORKING PROFESSIONALS:</u> It is seen that working professionals approach salary at extremes- they either shy away from talking a higher increment or talks about skyrocketed salary hikes. In a normal scenario, I would advise you to quote a number at around 45% higher than your fixed salary and after a round of negotiation you might settle at around 30-35%. In cases where fixed salary is less and bonus/ incentives/variables form a large part of your salary, it is advisable to quote in terms of total in-hand salary and the decent hike on the total take-home salary only. Now the term 'decent hike' will have different meaning for different companies and industries for which you might write to us via mail, and we will guide you as per your job profile/industry or discuss with the professionals who are already working in the same profile in similar companies to understand the market rates/ benchmarks.

TIME TO WIN

ALL THE BEST! GRAB YOUR DREAM JOBS!

End Of Book-not Learning!

I am glad that you have completed the book and reached to the end part. This is the end of this Personal Interview Module but learning ideally has no end.

Forward the link to buy this book to as many people as possible, your small contributions can impact many!

I tried covering most of the topics here and in case you feel you are prepared and want to give a mock, visit www.attitudematterz.com and book a slot for mock interview.

You may read our A2Z Handbook series on Group Discussion, Guesstimates, Consulting case preparation and Digital Marketing.

Attitude matterZ wishes you all the best for your future endeavours!